Hats Are the Enemy of Poetry

poems by

Bill Rector

Finishing Line Press
Georgetown, Kentucky

Hats Are the Enemy of Poetry

Copyright © 2021 by Bill Rector
ISBN 978-1-64662-390-7 First Edition
All rights reserved under International and Pan-American Copyright Conventions. No part of this book may be reproduced in any manner whatsoever without written permission from the publisher, except in the case of brief quotations embodied in critical articles and reviews.

ACKNOWLEDGMENTS

The following poems have been previously published, sometimes in different form or with a different title.

"Six apologies to William Blake;" 8 Poems
"The stage;" *2Rivers*
"Emily Dickinson is not in. Please leave a message;" "The platform;" *Apple Valley Review*
"Before;" *The Blue Nib*
"Last lecture;" *Fast Forward*
"One room schoolhouse;" "Conversation with a poet;" *Field*
"Every day;" "Do you know what you want;" "Far away is Mt. Fuji;" *Gyroscope Review*
"Album;" "Great opening;" "Three views of Memorial Day;" *Hotel Amerika*
"Elegy for anonymous;" *New Ohio Review*
"Rise and shine your shoes;" *Rhino*

Publisher: Leah Huete de Maines
Editor: Christen Kincaid
Cover Art: Bill Rector
Author Photo: Nancy Rector
Cover Design: Elizabeth Maines McCleavy

Order online: www.finishinglinepress.com
also available on amazon.com

Author inquiries and mail orders:
Finishing Line Press
PO Box 1626
Georgetown, Kentucky 40324
USA

Table of Contents

One Room Schoolhouse

Emily Dickinson is not in. Please leave a message 1
Conversation with a poet 2
Six apologies for William Blake 3
One room schoolhouse 5
Great opening 6
My father's shoes 7
Three views of Memorial Day 8
Out of Eden 9

It's for You

Hats are the enemy of poetry 13
It's for you 14
Night music 15
One hand clapping 16
The Laughing Heart 17
Elegy for anonymous 19
Album 20
Far away is Mt. Fuji 21

Rise and Shine Your Shoes

The stage 25
The platform 26
The last lecture 27
Overhead announcement 28
Rise and shine your shoes 29
Every day 30
Do you know what you want? 31
Before 32

One Room Schoolhouse

Emily Dickinson is not in. Please leave a message.

I dwell in possibility...

How does one escape from an upstairs window—?
And how far can one stray while remaining
in the childhood bedroom—?

On Madagascar, the world's smallest
chameleon has been discovered.

Such finds are a regular occurrence
on that remote island,
like family arguments, forest fires,
and religious holidays.

                                      The new chameleon
fits on the winding stem of a watch—.
Follows the road of the part in the hair—.
Pauses on a seismometer's trembling arm—.
        Hesitates like an eyelash on the unlit

head of a match—. At once streaking and
motionless, the comet-like creature
dashes from lines that would

describe it.
Barely a speck of ink
on the whorl of a fingertip,
vapor trail of a forgotten dream,
the newest chameleon is best seen
with a jeweler's loupe in a full moon's eye.

How was it discovered? What are we afraid of?

Conversation with a poet

Morning mist rises from the pond like fine gray hair.

A deer watches from the forest's edge. Is it safe?

Ten years after the Holocaust, Tadeusz Rozewicz wrote:

> Forget us
> Forget our generation

I mention you, Tadeusz, only because this morning an anthology fell open to these lines.

The spine wanted me to read you. The cracked glue of the binding inspired me.

Where the deer stood
is a cold hearth.

A few white logs.
A sooty swirl of ravens.

You didn't mean what you wrote. Few do.
You meant to say:

> Remember us
> Remember our generation

The mist is gone.

Six apologies to William Blake

Ah, sunflower, weary of time,
I prefer your name in French,

le tournesol. It so perfectly
matches what you are,

you could almost be a verb.
Je tournesol matin et soir…

          ***

Ah, sunflower, weary of time,
it's a little creepy, honestly,

to watch you turn east,
then west, like a living watch

worn on a living wrist,
so the sun can tell the time.

          ***

Ah, sunflower, weary of time,
I find that your crown

is not of petals, but flowers
that resemble petals,

the way a logarithm
has a number above its head.

          ***

Ah, sunflower, weary of time,
you are, in my experience,

like Mickey Mouse pointing
at me instead of ten and two,

and squeaking, Time's up!
you innocent child, you.

***

Ah, sunflower, weary of time,
don't you get a little bored,

examining the line of the horizon
from dawn to dusk, looking for,

if not an answer, a different way
to frame the question?

***

Ah, sunflower, weary of time,
and the margins of the field,

and the highway passing through,
and farmhouses' broken windows,

and the hissing of the snake,
the locust, and the mole…

One room schoolhouse

The ranch house triples as Post Office and General Store. What ever happened to that inviting lie—Gone Fishing? **We Can't Make Change for Every Body Who Stops Here, So That Means No One!** By the smudge under the exclamation point, the Magic Marker had run dry. The sign on the soft drink machine humming on the dusty porch warns there isn't any more Mountain Dew, anyway. The sun's almost down behind the hogback. *Are we there yet?* Yes. No. *Go back to sleep.* Crickets have begun sawing on the fine links between the l's of the willows along Horse Creek, the dark t's of the broken cattails. There's a globe on the teacher's tiny desk, drawings of seahorses, stranger than angels, on the walls. Dark clattering hooves... a comet a hands-breadth above the silhouette of a mountain... this was before the wanderings, when it was possible to put the head down and sleep unnoticed. Barbed wire and mule deer antlers go on woolgathering under the stars. Were I told, Dig a tunnel to China, this is where I would begin.

Great opening

The skull of a pronghorn antelope floats on my palm, as light and delicate as a balsawood raft. Smooth at the top, the horns grow rough at the base, twin candles that have guttered partway down on a sloping sill of bone. The prongs point forward, but the tips, being older (one is broken off), rear back. The dome and horns make me think of a *chapeau de fou*, the original of Yorick's cap. Turned over, the skull presents a different aspect, an abandoned cliff-village, a calcified honeycomb. Symmetrically-paired nerve openings mimic the pattern of spots on the wings of an Atlas moth. I raise the spinal opening to an eye. Through the telescope of bone, whose tube held the brain and whose aperture is the sockets, I can see the leafless pear tree in the front yard, my car asleep under a dusting of snow, and the breath-plumed mailman striding up the drive, letters in hand. Latin stirs in my temporal lobe, together with a pungent whiff of formalin exhaled by my cadaver in medical school:

Foramen magnum.

My father's shoes

His feet were bare. I don't know why
I recall this detail first among others,
but I do. That, and his twisted posture
and wide eyes, as though he was shocked
at being seized so roughly in the night
and thrown back carelessly on the bed.

It shames me to remember him so,
in a scene of mortal humiliation,
but I do. That and my surprise
at having so easily crossed a threshold
I'd only half-understood was there.
At the door, his feet looked back at me.

Three views of Memorial Day

Walls, floats. Windows tubas, colliding symbols, drums. Outstretched arms, trombones. Quite soon it's over. No one's immune to the rash. Newspapers, blustery wind. A clown hurries to a toy car.

***

Extinct aurochs drawn in ocher and torch smoke. Skull of cave bear. Altar of rock. Shaman-figure above the stone niche, which can only be reached by small boys. One eye is huge, the other small.

***

At eye-level on the butcher's counter, a shallow steel pan with the brains. *Bacon, Chops, Sausage.* Slabs of ribs gleaming where the bone was cut. Paper doilies… on each a strangely dainty ankle, neatly folded hoof.

Out of Eden

To sink from the eternal into the human
cannot be described in words.

Break off a branch.
Draw a squiggle in the dust of the road.

It happens so fast,
it's like running over a snake with your car.

It's For You

Hats are the enemy of poetry

> *Words are the enemy of poetry.*
> —Russell Edson

When folks rub their heads and ask what my poems are about, I describe my collection of hatboxes. One resembles a library globe, with seven continents and seven seas, except it has a handle like a suitcase. Another is indistinguishable, even to a flag that goes up and down, from the mailbox at the end of my drive, where rejection notices arrive. A third may be mistaken by browsers for a birch bark canoe, or a quarter moon afloat upon the clearness of an evening.

Some of you may not be satisfied, so let me tell it in a different way.

When I find a hatbox that I admire, I first shake it firmly to be certain there's nothing inside. Then—call me crazy—I place it on my head, or atop the hatboxes I am already wearing. Sometimes a ladder is required. Before you go (for time is forever setting off without us), try the round one emblazoned with a ruddy sunset for size. It may prove too small, perched on your head like a felt thimble, or too large, falling over your eyes like a blindfold, hiding everything.

Or the fit might be right, and you'll admit, *This fellow has style.*

It's for you.

I have made the smile of Mona Lisa
the ring-tone on my new cellular phone.

Now, when I am next in line to shake
the hand of the President of France, or the film

has reached the point where hero and heroine
discover what is obvious to all, they are in love,

or heads begin to sink into yawning caverns
in the Reading Room, frowns at the unwanted

intrusion of one life into another will be replaced
by sudden recognition and shared wonder:

Hello! And because you call those who hear
with the smile that is your silence, I will not answer.

Night music

As children, we took violin lessons from Albert Einstein. Remember? He didn't ask for miracles or even proper scales. He didn't care what we played as long as our instruments were in tune. The orchestra was assigned a composition called, "The Twentieth Century." But when it came time to perform, there wasn't a score, the maestro didn't appear, and the auditorium had been rented by a Star Trek convention. Most of the performers donned masks and disappeared in the crowd. Perhaps you did, too. Or is that you at the far end of the stage, also faithful to an assignment you never fully understood, rubbing your rough wings together for those mock-solemn listeners, the stars and moon?

One hand clapping

The head leper, the hardest to look upon,
with coarse features like a balding lion,
steps forward. He has a deep voice
from nights spent arguing with the moon.

He tells a sweet story about his grandkids.
Lepers are incurably sentimental.
And they like their sentiment overdone,
the sloppier the better.

Along with sob stories, lepers are fond of jokes
they tell about one another. Unlike us,
lepers prefer their punch lines in the gut.
In their experience, it's more real.

The laughter of lepers is highly infectious.
If even one leper starts to laugh,
the whole colony is soon rolling around
like 8-balls on a merry go round.

But truly, the moon has wept too much already.

The Laughing Heart

> *I contain multitudes.*
> —Walt Whitman

It happened like this. I was lying in a hammock,
pondering the last poems of Charles Bukowski,
when a UFO went by. It was a crappy hammock,
woven of fraying rope. It held me like a cocoon
that hung down so far my butt almost touched
the ground. Half of me wondered if I'd ever get
up again, while the other half examined the holes
in my jeans and wondered what has become of
the poems, as numberless as hangovers, sidewalk
afternoons, and stars, that Bukowski wrote, a
question that sort of answered itself, which led
me to wonder how long my poems will last,
and I decided, Not long, if at all, since I favor
moonshine, and poetry today is sipped like heart
medication, when I saw that what I'd taken for
a flying saucer was fireflies blinking in sequence,
like the signs spelling out MOTEL and COCK
TAILS on the highway into town. Even though
the lights weren't portholes of a flying saucer
like I'd thought, they lent wings to my spirits,
and I decided, even though I'm not what you'd
call a believer, that fireflies are a flashing sign
that there's something larger than us out there,
sending messages and offering a gentle kind of
order, plus a different way of looking at things,
eyelashes on butterflies, and maybe, just maybe,
keeping track of poetry no one reads, which
would be a great job for a super-smart race
of aliens that is moving unseen among
us and wants to understand how human
beings look at things. When I straightened
for a better look, the jug of liquor fell from
my lap and made the hammock flip, and the
ground flew up and knocked the wind out of

me, leaving me flat on my back, trying to catch
my breath, thinking, Holy Crap, I'm gonna die,
or at least throw up, while feeling around for
the flashlight under too many stars to count,
when I realized it wasn't earth I was on, but
a fire-ant hill, and as I leapt and swatted my
butt and ran out of my pants, and then my
underwear, a dog started howling by the trailer
in the woods, like it couldn't decide if it wanted
to be lonely or hungry, or both at the same time.

Elegy for anonymous

> *Do you not see how necessary a world of pain and troubles is to school an intelligence and make it a soul?*
> —John Keats

I never met the Dean of the Medical School. What I remember most about him is a memo on mortality, posted to the faculty not long after I arrived. He'd fallen ill, heart failure, and was surrendering his duties. He framed his profession and his life as a braid that had become knotted at the end. Unheard-of candor for a doctor. And not bad poetry. After he died, a portrait appeared outside the Office of Admissions. He balances a featureless globe in one hand and holds a stethoscope loosely in the other. The building is old and annually redone. The main corridor jogs left, right, then left again, ending between two hospital wings in a plaza where, in the spring, spindly lilacs bring forth fragrant asterisks and graduation ceremonies are held. The stethoscope I understand. I don't get the globe. Students hurry past, heavy volumes pressed to their chests. *We fashion a pattern for our lives*, the memo concluded. *Then we find ourselves inside.*

Album

After the rain stopped, I felt cooped-up, so I took my camera for a walk. It tugged on its leash like a puppy for which the world is new, pointing its black nose at everything in sight. We stopped at a low wall in the shade of some bearded oaks. The stones would not let us explore further, however fiercely the shutter clicked. The topmost were like vertebrae of a fantastic animal that no longer visits the surface. But it was alive, purring as I ran my palm over the gray-green lichen of the pelt, remembering its builders' long-ago touch. The double life of the stones, among men and earth, made me think of the marine spirals found in the building blocks of the Great Pyramid at Giza, fingerprints from the Eocene Period mingling with quarry marks of a later era. White ibises were feeding among glistening puddles in a nearby field. They're ridiculous-looking birds, rocking up and down like bobble-head toys as they hurry this way and that, pecking the mud with their long beaks. I remembered watching, at another time and place, a heron standing on one leg in a shallow pond, when something clicked behind my eyes, and the motionless bird became a water pump with a long handle. When I raised the camera, the flock flew off in formation, a school of tropical fish in a lagoon of air.

Far away is Mt. Fuji.

> *You are wise to climb Mt. Fuji,*
> *but a fool to do it twice.*
> *—Japanese proverb*

Let us replace
contemplation of the ideal
with consideration of the human.

Let us speak for a moment, if no
longer, about lightning,
not those forking bolts beyond

our power to command or recreate,
but rather their after-images, our own fading
memories, and the incomprehensible

language of thunder. How are we to translate
the world's message into words?
As if summoned by our questioning,

our ignorance, writing
descends like rain from the sky.
A few of the characters resemble limbs

of a wind-tortured pine, others, blown-
apart bones of a hut (chromosomes
in mid-mitosis) or scudding

leaves and bits of roof-straw, being
drawn into the grip
of a great wave about to break.

Rise and Shine Your Shoes

The stage

Bringing the microphone to attention, Czeslaw
Milosz reads his poem, "Encounter," in Polish.
The Laureate from another land then boards
the wooden wagon of English to read it again.
After that, he recites the poem in sign language.
He points at the sky and then at the ground.
Taps letters on the lectern in Morse code.
The horse's hooves clop; the hare dashes.
He recites the poem in complete silence
to an empty auditorium. For an encore,
he removes his hat, an old cloth one, and pulls
a rabbit from it. The rabbit runs a little ways
on the stage, then stops and looks back.

The platform

Built into our cell
phones and the fabric
of the Cloud and glowing
in our dashes as we navigate

the night is a program
that updates where we are,
directions to our destination,
and the way back home again.

Pull over.
Take off your hat.
Look at the evening sky.

Pilgrim, have you lost your way?

Or have you waited so long
for your journey to begin
that when your eyes open
in the morning, now

and then are a single word?
As though calipers of starlight
touched your temples while
you slept, and the distance

from birth was measured?
The Twenty-first Century
Limited flashes past,

headed in the opposite direction.

Last lecture

I have been a physician longer than you students have been alive. How distant the future must seem. How eager you are for it to arrive! How much more my gray head must seem to hold than yours. I talk too much. I always have, but less now. Young friends, nascent colleagues, caretakers of my advancing years, I confess that I have forgotten nearly everything that I once knew. I have passed so far beyond Introductory Physics that I approach weightlessness. I have spun the objective of Beginning Biology beyond the highest power and now find myself returning my own, magnified stare. I have passed multiple-choice tests in which no answer is true and done so with perfect scores. I have done this again and again. You will, too. You will do everything I say. It will happen before you know it. Gray rain of the ceiling, white dew on the desk.

Overhead announcement

A sparrow pecks crumbs
of departed passengers.
A fly waits like a miniature
jet on a runway of glass.

Travelers look haunted.
Faces are cracked visors.
Arrivals and departures
scroll beneath their lids.

What you know about yourself
that you've told no one,
not even God, is who you are.

Blessed are those who do not
have baggage. On this flight,
the overhead bins will be full.

Rise and shine your shoes

Last year, I woke up
every morning
with size 67 feet.

Make that 68.

A tiny figure
is scaling the
twin, sheeted Alps
at the end of the bed.

While I slept,
he crossed
the foothills
of the ankle
and the ridges
of the metatarsals.

Now the miniature
mountaineer
nears the summit.

He looks older. Bowed.
Grayer than I remember.

He who built sand castles
and flew on the wings of books
must attempt the steepest ascent yet:

the sheer cliff of the right great toe.

He carries a tiny flag.
Or perhaps it's a lily.
It's hard to see clearly.

I wiggle my toe.

Down he tumbles, vanishing into a wrinkle.

Every day

The cliffs of Ireland are being wiped
away like a child's chalk drawing
by the wet eraser of the sea.

Cirrus clouds fletch their fraying
to fresh contrails to arrow
the way from Dublin to Boston.

Headstones, so lichen-
mottled they appear to have been
dusted for fingerprints,

tilt this way and that, dozing
parishioners in turfy pews,
or rest upon the ground,

footprints of wandering spirits.
In a far corner is one freshly-cut,
smooth but for its legend:

Seamus Heaney: 1939-2013
　Walk On Air Against
　Your Better Judgment.

Not a long span by modern standards,
but long enough. The wind
has picked up. It's hard to stand against.

The vault wants us back, and one day we'll go.

Do you know what you want?

In the time it takes me to reply, *Angel*
Hair Pasta with White Wine Sauce and a Garden

Salad with Raspberry Vinaigrette, the waiter
jots a poem on his small, lined pad.

How I envy the thoughtless ease
of his composition. Had I been told,

before I sat down here with you,
write a poem for your supper,

I'd still be at the kitchen table.
I'd be picking my teeth with the pencil.

I'd be warming up left-overs.
The young man asks expectantly,

Will That Be All? and takes his little
work to the kitchen for the cook to see.

Before

Hummingbirds, Sweetheart,
there was plutonium.
Before plutonium,
hummingbird

tongues, as quarks
are called in this poem, were all
the rage. Before quarks,
and rage, and sorrow, there was tohu

bohu, which is not, Thank Heaven,
sushi made from tofu and tears,
which probably does exist
somewhere on this unhappy

planet, but language from
Genesis, which I read as feathers
of every color flying in all
directions at once from a prior

destruction, which at a touch
reassemble as a hummingbird
of every color hovering before
a honeysuckle blossom

in the garden of a God
we do not, cannot, comprehend,
for what seems more than
an instant, but less than eternity.

Bill Rector is a physician who retired from practice in Denver and now lives in South Carolina with his wife, who is also a retired physician. He has published one full-length poetry collection, entitled *bill*, and four chapbooks. These include: *Lost Moth*, about the loss of his daughter, which won the *Epiphany* magazine chapbook competition; *Biography of a Name* (Unsolicited Press), relating the death of Jimmy Hoffa to contemporary American culture; *Brief Candle* (Prolific Press), a series of sonnets in modern idiom about selected characters from Shakespeare; and *Two Worlds* (White Knuckle Press), relating the transcendent to the ordinary, which the editors called one of the most beautiful collections they have published.

www.ingramcontent.com/pod-product-compliance
Lightning Source LLC
LaVergne TN
LVHW041601070426
835507LV00011B/1229